Loves' Simplicity

Poetry: Thoughts of Sweet Epiphanies

Loves' Simplicity

JaNae A. Carter

Dedication:

First and foremost I thank my Heavenly Father for which All Blessings flow from. I dedicate this book to my Father, my Daddy Earl Carter, Sr. who passed 3 years ago on May 16, 2012.

I am so humbled to finally get my gift out in the open, it has been a long time coming. Family, friends, and all that know me…. I truly am thankful for the support and love.

Thank You.

Table of Contents:

Hair Worth:

It's a journey yes, but in that moment we find ourselves.

We are to not seek definition, but to know simply our worth.

Naturalness is pure, it's worth saving, preserving....its joy is fulfilling.

See, the worth is more then what the eye can see, it can't be covered up with the sentiments of society's disillusion in a magazine, or a runway.

We must not mask it with how society wants us to be, but embrace who we are internally and externally.

The patience is in its growth, it is the progress that makes me smile.

The journey is real, the Freedom is Beautiful...the Growth is Astounding.

Hair....Simply Hair....I Adore You!

The Naturalness is Tedious, but the journey, the journey is oh so Rewarding...Simplicity at its best.

Nights' Thoughts......

THE Simplest thing is that we fear the unknown.... but how about a release because you know what, Change Is inevitable.

We figure why we haven't moved on to that next level, but God is simply making us see that we have not learned while we're in the situation, but we want out so bad.

Growth and Understanding is the key.

Patience needs to be practiced daily to see the bigger picture.

Life is too short, let us embrace it fully and wholeheartedly with respect to knowing that it's what we Need that's ahead, and not what we want.

We dream of better, greater; the Reality must not scare us....Believe and Trust GOD!

Stubbornness Evades Me.....

I simply won't be able to stop so suddenly loving him.

Nope, I won't be able to suddenly stop thinking about him.

Hmm...If my feelings, my heart was a faucet would I then turn it off knowing I can with one simple turn?

The complexity of this is that sometimes the optimism is stronger than the situation...

I won't simply be able to just stop caring within a week, two weeks, a month, etc.

Simply loving an Imperfectly Perfect person beyond flaws is the sheer will to simply Love.

I'm not sure why I still have hope, my stubbornness, maybe I'm naive??

I simply won't be able to not want to pick the phone up and call, laugh, share, love...all this came so effortlessly.

I simply will have to keep so busy, that at the end of a day I smile. Not because of the good day but I made it through a day of no tears.

"Impregnate"

No first response needed, No waiting around for the deeds of the night before to consume my thoughts, my consciousness is already bothered, already under attack and I can't wait!

See there's no need for me to go to the pharmacy, hand them that doctors script for the "morning after pill", for me to wait on Mother Nature to let me know one way or the other, should I be obligated to her?

What will be, shall and the decisions will always require responsibility and let us gather the true sense of this being as options are weighed.

Impregnate me NOT with what you thought I was talking about Lol...But with Truth, with Life, with Love, with purpose, humbleness, and so much more of all that God needs me to be. See God has already instilled in me which I do solemnly seek.

Impregnated with Newness beyond my comprehension.

True Intentions

With such simplicity I love and with the essence that's within I stand humbled and revel in Gods amazing glory.

See as time passes I am a soul, learning and growing to see what exactly Gods purpose is for my Life.

Settle, yes I have but Father allow me not to ANYMORE, allow me to strive for greatness, allow Love to surpass my understanding amongst the insanity, simply Allow your grace and mercy to cover my present/Future endeavors. Yep, #InLoveWithMyFuture# tatted and felt wholeheartedly.

For our meaning is not known, try to grasp and it's misconstrued, misconceived, misunderstood.

I respectfully resolve All issues and execute the Will set forth from my Father and simply, dutifully...Love.

My True stance is LOVE...breathing it, seeing it, experiencing it pass the pain, pass the insanity, simply pass my circumstances....I choose Love.

Positive Energy.......

Love......one of Gods' greatest emotions. I cannot fathom it at times, but I so embrace it first from my Father who sees me and accepts me even in my progression, even when I'm messing up and trying to get to my Beautiful future!

See, dig this the simplicity is All laid out, there waiting, to be embraced and cherished for a Lifetime.
Love you....Is Loving Me. As I Love I smile unconsciously, under its control, I'm under its spell...hmm L O V E...right? Lol
God IS Love....Let's just remember that distance does not make Love dissipate....It only makes it stronger!

Reflection = Growth=Simplicity=Love.

I have learned in Life, Nothing is a guarantee. Learning now at the start of this New Year I have things I need to work on! Letting go of all insecurities that cause me to second guess! I will not let the enemy come in and cause friction with my future! See I'm so vehemently in Love with my Future and it will be Beautiful then I ever imagined. I am flawed in some areas, but I will not let that deter me from what God has in store. Looking on the inside and asking God to take away anything that may hinder my future...qualities I see now must be deleted to become a better me! ❤

The Bus Ride to Reality!

Yes the walk is exhibited daily starting approximately @ 12:15 between 1:00pm....a simple casual stroll straightening up items, productively and repetitiously taking the much needed time to make sure Nothing is overlooked. A simple walk here, a simple walk there until the very moment when the walk becomes a fiasco of literally throwing people under the bus!

See the derogatory name calling, the questions as to why subordinates act out, the sneakiness of a straight face when all along it was a bluff! It has led to unnecessary measures being taken that my "security" has been compromised! Help me, Help me....out this cesspool that has sunk into an abyss of.....Nothingness.

See dig this.....the glaring eyes back and forth and the unnecessary chatter leads me to think that this really is what your characters are made of and the conscious decision to drop names, judge, and allow smugness to take root is unbelievable beyond comprehension.

This walk merely includes 3 to 4 people at a time all with their own opinions, but the ride to this Reality has jolted to a complete Stop and I want to get off, money has been rendered....steps down, I walk as I exit and take it all in!

Moments......

See dig this moments can be repeated but why when there's always time to create new ones?!

See.... It's the moment when I saw you and said what if?

The moment when I realized Wow!

It was the very moment stamped in time when unconsciously I said what my heart is in fear of!

I'm experiencing these moments and All the past hurts seem to be so irrelevant ....hmmm I ponder!

The moments are becoming clear, are becoming imaginable to this ol' heart of mines....

See dig this I've been reluctantly hearing what YOU might become to me....but I hear and just let it marinate because the journey to it was already written by God.

Simple Concept......

Yes everyone has their own way of showing love, being in love, loving the concept of Love And All the elements.....But see dig this are some ready for the experience of Love, the turmoil that it may possibly bring, the good times along with a little bad mixed in?

With such a concept to take control of mind, body, and soul....are you ready, will you be?

See dig this is there something wrong with me that my unadulterated Love may possibly be what you are afraid of?

I don't know how someone can be afraid of something so Beautiful, unless it's just not with me!?

See dig this that the mere understanding requires the Truth and for some reason I

Can't get it!

4 letters...1 meaning.....

I'm amazed at you sometimes

You're something that I always talk about.....you seem to capture the deepest vessels that only God knows about.

How did you become a part of my world from day one?

I truly never want to lose you in this life that I've been so generously given.

From the depths of my soul I'm asking you to stay, to start over, and to just see me as I see you.

Lol... I know forever can be Beautiful with you.

Life jacket.....

I've been in this ocean for too long now.

This ocean seems to know me personally.

Vast in area and deep in size and yet it has me swallowed up.

I'm here trying to escape and I see no life jacket in sight.

I'm trying to catch my breath and still I'm grasping for air.

Water is entering my mouth, flashes of moments, and I'm trying to stay afloat...please God help!

In a breath, paddling to reach and grab a hold to something, someone.....No One is there!

My mind is oblivious to that I know how to swim, but in that one moment I was taken away with the currents of this ocean made simply of.......Love.

Riddle me this.....Who are you???

You negated to let me know that this would be tedious.

You negated to tell me that this process would be to the extreme that I question myself.

I sit back and wait that the "one" that chooses you will be True, Honest, respectful, loving, caring, passionate and so much more.

I'm wondering do you really know what you want, or is this a waste of your time and mines.

See...truth speaking I know what you want and I'm here.

I've been with you when you've cried, when you were broken, when your trust was compromised because you cared a little too much.....I was there!

LOL....I'm here now and I need you to TRUST and hold tight because your Father got U!

I know, I know that you only let people in that you trust, they might misuse that(be prepared)...that you are perplexed right now, do you have the green light to say how you feel and will it be reciprocated? You don't know, I don't either!

I have said ALL this to say that....I'm here and I'm pulling for you, I feel for you, I give you that feeling, I know who you love deeply, I want the very best for you...You deserve "him", your King, don't settle, don't share, just be you, let them fall for you, let them See YOU, let this journey that you're so anxious for be about the right instead of always about the wrong because they Negated to tell you you're not the "only one"!

I Love You. I got you. Yours will come. TAKEN won't be just a movie!

WHO AM I??? Your heart, JaNae.

SECONDS: In time you're thought of.

Second: the smallest unit in time.

Taking time out in this micro of a second to reflect on the pure essence of you.

Taking time out to have the pleasure in just knowing you.

Yes....I miss you, I smile when you're thought upon and still I reflect.

How loyal I am to you and ALL that you represent in truth and GOD!

You define life itself and the exact moment that I met you....lol *blushing*.

You... I am descriptive about and the mere thought process is quite disturbed because you are just that Over-Whelming!

They say you are the driving force, the accelerant that puts everything in motion.....you are Genius!!

Taking an Immediate, yet potential, crucial, stand in time to just.....wait for you!

LOVE.

My him....

See I'm trying to get to know you, wanting to know your in's and out's, trying to know what you like what you dislike, what you may like on that sandwich, what your taste buds just delight in if they taste it and get the simplest smell of it.

See I want to be so comfortable with you and around you that technically we are and will become each other's best friends. See I want you to find rest in me, and know that when your days, well our days become over whelming I'm definitely there to listen as you are. See Love is what my Father gave to me SO Vehemently and He let me know that it's okay to share it with that" one" that will truly appreciate and know that just because I'm here....True Love does exist!!!

I carry No falsehoods, No lies, No deceitfulness that will break your heart, No cruel intentions that will leave a stain upon how you perceive me to be....See I'm just trying to leave a lasting impression of my Love, I'm trying to Never leave your heart once I get the opportunity to have the key.

Yes...this will just be common minds thinking alike to achieve one goal and that's to one day declare the Love we've found in front of our Father. See I don't know you, I might have met you, you may be in my life, I may have passed you and talked with you briefly and Never even knew, but my heart picked up on it.....but I await your arrival!!!

See my Father is preparing Me for you, I'm praying for you daily that your day to day activities are full of success, that the worries of this world does not consume you and that Love is shared in your heart and exuded.

A Dream slightly deferred?

Thinking that when something is deferred it is postponed, and or delayed. Can one be so stuck on love and the ideal of love that any other notion is obsolete, and giving up is never a thought?

Stuck: set in one place, grounded, rooted, not easily broke apart. What about when love has taken you through the turns, the trials, the tests, some you pass, some you fail...defeat does not and shall not have what's not obtainable right now, but patience is the key, contentment is the key to just accept and wait. Hmmm...True love deferred?? NEVER...Waking up and it will be a reality?

Simple Honesty.

Your Truth, my Truth is wrapped up in the pure tightness of the warmth that the simplest, most tender hugs brings.

See your Truth, your love is evident in the moments that I think of you and then I reflect that I have already known you and have gotten a glimpse of you.

See I sit back and reflect as I have been through things....but my Father let every test become my **TESTIMONY**!

I type this with the knowledge of knowing that my heart is beating and discovering itself, discovering the deliverance, the love, and the right that it has to simply LOVE TRUE and FREE without HURT!

See I am reluctant to look at you or think about you for longer than I have to because I can't fathom why my Father would bless me with you and you me.

See my darling I'm so excited in the purest notion that God blessed me to fall in love with you and to keep this repetitious moment happening for the rest of our lives! Wow....a never ending love story for ALL to see, and know that my Father above allowed this, at such a precise time that it's just so......

See I'm not concerned about your faults, not concerned who you've had before me...what matters now is that right here in this moment my heart has found yours and we have agreed to Love each other as Gods' word declares.

See I'm smiling writing this, because I know that you are somewhere so deserving of True Love...My love and upon Gods' promise, you and I won't have to wait much longer!!

THANK YOU FOR WHAT IT IS Now!!

I may not be in my own, but Thank You for what I have now!

I may not have my career, but Thank You for what it is now!

I may can't give my babies all what I need to, but Thank YOU for what's given now!

I may be slow understanding this walk, may stray, but Thank You for the light becoming brighter!

I may not have a clue, and things confuse me, but Thank You for peace.

I may not grasp situations or people, but Thank You for another day to learn.

I may still have flaws, but Thank You cause I'm a work in progress.

I may not have that "one", but Thank You God I'm be ready mentally & physically real soon.

I may at times have only $5.00 to my name, but Thank You for giving me that.

I may be consumed by this INFALLIBLE gift of Love, but I THANK You GOD for letting me breath it, have it flowing and daily configuring its plan in my purpose.

I may only be JaNae Arneisha Carter, but THANK You for the desire to be better 4 GOD, myself, my kids, my family, my friends, & my future husband.

I may not have much, but all I do have is because of Him...THANK YOU GOD!!!

Who was I before Him??

I wonder who I was before I met U, thoughts come to mind but they are faded.

Wondering who I'll be once I'm in the midst of you.

Just wondering.

I'm wondering about how you changed me, and rearranged me.

Yep, I'm just wondering is this a dream that I have not awaken from.

A fallacy of an imagination that I want to be true but is beyond my comprehension.

I'm just wondering how I ever lived without you!!!

I was missing you without even truly knowing you.

Just wondering how I managed without you. Without you...smh now that's scary!

I'm wondering who I'll be with you and my heart forever smiles....

Just wondering about Him...yes U Jesus!

Whom God has.....My husband!

Hey....I just wanted to tell you that I think about you. I dream of what your face will be like, what characteristics that you will possess that will have me automatically knowing that **YOU** were sent by *GOD!* Hey...I just wanted to tell you that you consume the very vessels that *God* created for you to inhabit. Funny thing is that it was especially designed for you and only you...so beautiful was this concept that my Creator thought of. So beautiful to know that I want you right there by my side as I worship, as you worship and together just giving praise to the Creator on high!! Standing side by side and forever encouraging each other along the way. Hey...I just wanted to tell you that I cannot wait for the privilege to love you for the rest of my life. Knowing that *God* is first and I your Queen and ours will be the focus and none other. **NO** other detractions will break this union that *God* himself put together....Oh what a day that'll be! When this, our love story was already predestined before you and I were even thought about! Letting you know that ALL my past relationships, ALL yours has brought us to this point ...**No REGRETS**...I cherish because if it wasn't for them I wouldn't be strong and respectful of the fact that they did not ruin my idea of what **TRUE LOVE** can be and ALL that it will offer when *GOD* is **ALL** up and through the relationship first and foremost!

AS **Prov.18:22 says**: He that finds a wife, finds a good thing! Man that says it all...

I am humbly waiting until we met, may have already, he may already be within my life, but then him and I will see that this kind of love does exist when *God* has ordained it and called it to BE!!!

Well...just letting you know that this woman of *God* is waiting patiently for you, my heart will know that my *God* truly knew that I needed you in my life to share good times, bad times, laugh, cry, everything that is So beautiful in love.

It's funny that my eyes and heart will know you and only you. I will see you and my heart will smile with content that through ALL the heartache that you and I have been through that True unconditional Love truly does exist and I'm so thankful that it does....

2 WORLDS TORN APART......

Not knowing what to say...Not knowing how to feel

all that I know that this is surreal...

But I say now that GOD and only God is going to work this out...

My heart hurts for ALL that loved him, ALL that know her, and are asking why...but it really goes out to 2 children that will only have a memory of their father.

Shouldn't we all be concerned about that?

It takes MORE ENERGY TO HATE...THEN TO LOVE!!!!!

I pray that God swiftly heals the hearts of his family and make them whole....

No one should wish another soul burn in a place that will be HOT for ALL eternity....

ONLY GOD WILL DECIDE THIS.... on JUDGEMENT DAY!

I know that time heals ALL wounds and I pray, and hope that it will for everyone that's involved, for every family member of both, for ALL!!!

Domestic Violence HAS NO PLACE IN ANY RELATIONSHIP...but God has a reason and cause for everything....NO ONE SHOULD QUESTION THAT!

As days go day we all are going TO cry, are going to miss him, but GOD will give peace after this storm!

Greg... you may be gone but never forgotten. Protect your children on this earth and be with them and your loved ones always! your little man is a splitting image of you...He is so sweet but has that other side lol

I hope you know your son and daughter will have LOVE in their Life forever......

MY Sister....I LOVE YOU that will FOREVER BE!!!!

My heart can do nothing but LOVE...I'm a child of GOD, I am trying to make sense of this, my understanding is trying to become bigger then this Life, but I AM seeking my FATHER in this time.....PLEASE know people that HATRED, or MALICE has no place!!!

2 worlds torn apart....but GOD WILL SHOW HIS SELF NOT HATE n heal these 2 families....

Gods' Will never take U where God's grace can't protect U....and with that said this 2 shall past!!!

I AM THE BEST....So grateful!!

Such a Great God... to see a simple person such as myself as the BEST!

He's mine and I'm his... he only sees me for who I AM!

I'm Me, but He gets ME, understands me, consoles me....He loves me in spite of.

I...so grateful beyond anyone's comprehension!

Crying...because I'm HIS...I can be me and accepted without judgement!

So Beautiful....Jesus to be loved beyond human emotions by YOU!!!

So imperfect and with flaws am I...but HE, He sees the best when everyone else saw the worst!

When people wrote Me off, said I would never make it, used Me, Abused Me physically and emotionally and did not value my love, ME...God's purpose was Greater, He rescued Me from when the enemy wanted to destroy Me!!! He knew that one day my love will count! Smh...Soo grateful...so blessed...don't know what to do but CRY....Thank YOU FATHER!

To be created in His image...smh I'm trying to live right... the Best has to lol!

To be mines regardless of anything I've done....Oh Father you are Amazing!

Thank you for being Mines. For my precious children being mines...that's ALL I have...

No man will accept me for me only the one God sends me...I am the Best. I deserve the Best. My future will be the Greatest...I have a Father that reassures Me SO!

They are why I live!

They are why I live! They were my destiny.... for it was written they I would bear them. They are the meaning of my life, who I am, my affection, my whole understanding, my being, my LOVE and why I am so grateful for life! They are the reasons that I am a mother. They at the end of the day give me peace, reassurance, laughter, and LOVE! They are why I stay strong and not worry what others may say about my life. They are my 2 hearts.... the loves of my life; My Foreverloves! They are my trueness and my understanding why I'm on this earth. If and when I'm blessed with more.....God knows I would be grateful. They are everything, my heart beats only for them and not a MAN! They are why I strive to get to work, go to school, and better myself for their future! I want them to be proud to have me as a mother as I am proud and without comprehension to have them as my children! With my last breath I would say........ I'm so grateful to have been your mother.... God blessed me with ANGELS! They are why I live, why I fight in this day to day struggle, this vehement world, this nonsense makeup of reality...... they are why I live!

Domestic Violence!

But I LOVE You!

The first time that it happened I thought it was a mistake, but it wasn't. After that I heard, but I love you!

The second time it happened I thought, did I say something wrong? Maybe out the way? Then I heard, but I love you!

The third and fourth time that it happened I thought there is an issue here and why does he feel like this violent thing can be done against me? Then I heard, but I love you!

So on and so on it kept going, looking in the mirror not even recognizing the Black woman that I was. Turning away at the reflection for it was not me, but I still heard, But I Love you!

I loved him and it seemed that he hated me! Loved him, but he gave me rage! I gave my all and still it wasn't enough for his satisfaction.

I heard the I Love You's, the I need you's, the I can't live my life without you's, the it won't happen again's, the I apologize, ...but in still he said .. But I love you!

...But I LOVE YOU was the last words that I heard as I looked at him and said why? I looked over my life, thanked God for my years, my children, and my family, and sighed! He was still uttering, but I LOVE You!

Dedicated to those Women that have gone through Domestic Violence. Know that 1 time is enough, Love does not HURT!

MARRIAGE......

Proverbs 18:22....Simple: He that findeth a WIFE, finds what is good and receives favor from the Lord.

So this Dating thing...I'll pass!

See I've been plagued and intrigued at the same time...

I'm trying to know what it's about.

I hear that it's so much that occurs when two are joined together.

I watch couples from their 80's hold hands, to couples simply intertwine and dance in their love no matter who's watching.

A kiss stolen atop the forehead, kisses saturated on the neck, just to know that he is yours and you are his!

See...dig this I see it and I know that God will give you the desires of your heart.

I need that feeling of being overwhelmed when I don't just call him my Boyfriend, my fiancée, but my HUSBAND!

NO...it won't be perfect, I won't be, he won't be, but the ultimate goal is to create something so unique and divine that it will be cherished until out last breath...

Let me simply take part, Can I simply get a glimpse of what this might be?

Yes, I know that trials and tribulations will come but I plan to love him, US, OUR family, enough to get past it.

I want to come home simply knowing this is US and be what we build, sustain, and forever prayed on!!

Can you, someone, please tell me the disadvantages of this?

Lol...you can't there's is none!

Not perfect... just "Simply Being"

After the hurt and the pain subsides.

Imperfect but just wanted him to see me perfectly.

Love is forever even beyond Flaws.

Grass is not greener on the other side.

The wrongs can't be made right.

Misunderstanding can't be fixed.

Interest was slowly leaving.

Communication isn't the same.

You want things better, but not the same as the beginning.

I and my goodness have left a stain, good intentions become over doing.

Never meant to be toxic, extra...only meant to love, Simply Love.

Convinced that if love was real and true then excuses would not have been made.

A fight for love, for future, for substance, for growth, would have been stronger.

Perplexed, taken aback, Focused.

Lose to win huh?

Lose to Win!

"First Contact"

......text sent and he replied hey and from there begin the journey of the unknown. From the playful banter, to the sly remarks, to the unconscious flirting, to a love that was developing, simmering and I didn't even know it. He said walls would be broken down and unwittingly I did not believe such...but they did.
So it led to evenings out, characters shown, and with that this thing called love was becoming ours!
On such an intriguing night we talked, laughed, exchanged knowledge, next my ears was inclined to hear those words and I shed tears of unbelief.
I love You...words uttered and my heart smiled.
From there love in its simplest moments was ours.

Simple Love......

As we ride I looked over to my left and saw a man with so much potential. Door opens and we cascade in greeted with warmness. Seated with him on my right and eyes wide open. Partake in kisses so spontaneous. Smiles cover my face unexpectedly. Food so delicious to every bite taken. Devoured yet wanting more. Check paid, relishing our moment. Inhale, exhale nights air. Drive back and yet I stare in awe at how GOD blessed me. Lights passed. Gaze unbroken, heart flutters.

Such simplicity in our Love. In our days. Time always well spent. ❤

I Got My Boaz!

As I sit and contemplate this, I stand in awe! See God himself answered prayers and directed us to the moment that put us in the path of something wonderfully Great!

See dig this I thought I wasn't deserving, been messed over, lied to, deceived, but God had me go through ALL the Mr. wrongs just so my Boaz could find me!

I claimed it and now God is allowing me to experience something that's free of worries, free of lies, free of cheating, free of emotional and physical abuse....My GOD You are awesome beyond my comprehension!

THANKS....to ALL the MR. Wrong's!!!!

thank you to the ones that lied to me, thank you for the ones that underestimated my true intelligence, thank you to the ones that did not see my worth and tried me, thank you for the ones that made me to believe that I was the only one and this was going somewhere, thank you to the ones that said they weren't ready for a meaningful relationship and next minute they was in one,(they saved me and I just didn't know at the time...HA)thank you to the ones that convinced me that WE were in a relationship and next thing I know he got a child on the way(LOL), thank you to the ones that felt their manhood was in their pants and shared(I DONT SHARE) and in their FISTS, thank you for the ones that hurt me to my deepest roots, thank you to the ones that keep SO secretive when ALL I wanted to do was share their world and Love them UNCONDITIONALLY, thank you to the ones that did NOT call just to see how my day's was going, just to tell me they were thinking about me(I NEEDED A JUST BECAUSE), thanks to the ones that made me feel they cared but it was ALL a mirage, thanks to the ones that did reverse psychology to make it ALL my fault, thanks to the ones that didn't get a chance to know my heart(their lose), thanks to the ones that thought I'd NEVER CATCH ON.......

THANKS,THANKS, THANKS.....for not appreciating Me, my love, my heart, my time, my company my world, my smile, my EVERYTHING!

THEY have prepared me for MY KING and I'm so THANKFUL!!!

These Women Cry…But Who Hears?

I see your beauty and I see your grace.

I'm seeing that you were a fragile person, but yet your demeanor keeps you from showing others your true self!

See…I'm looking at you and I'm perplexed, what drove you to this point?

Why are you here amongst all this Beauty?

Yes, I see beauty that has been stripped away and nothing is left but a shell trying to survive daily.

What is it my sisters that keeps you afloat?

That moment that has been frozen in time…what went through the corridors of your mind?

The abuse, the name calling, the cheating, the lies, the manipulation, the betrayal, the other woman, the other babies, the whole other family, the physical beat downs brought upon your spirit….has lead you right here and me looking at you and wondering why? My heart hurts.

See….my sisters I know that you have left behind your families, your child(ren), your life, your whole mindset has changed and become fixed…and I'm sorry.

See…I look at ALL this beauty and know that if GODS' grace and mercy did not keep me……I could be here amongst this congregation of wrong paths taken and left with permanent consequences!! I could have had those moments and with that fraction of a second, my life could've changed…..BUT GOD!!!

My sisters I care. Yes I don't know your names, don't know why and what for but my heart is heavy and the cycle that has brought you here….I'm praying it STOPS!!!

Dating vs Courting.

Love does not consist in gazing at each other, but in looking together in the same direction.

Courting should only happen once and end in a life-long covenant relationship. Dating happens lots of times, and ends in many hurts, heartbreaks, scars.

In dating we hide all our faults to give a false impression about ourselves in order for the partner to keep liking us. We date to satisfy our own needs.

-Courtship is about open and honest exploration of each other's lives and families leading up to engagement and marriage.

The primary purpose of marriage is not to please us, but to serve God.

Once we're married, we recognize that certain things are sacred to our partner. Things such as co-habitation, kissing, intimate hugging, sex, and bringing up children. We should recognize that not only our physical body, but our emotions, even our spirits are dedicated to that partner, for the rest of our life.

We cannot "touch" what does not yet belong to us. Only marriage relinquishes ownership of one's "good" body to one's partner.

Romans13:10.

Metamorphosis

Yep...before I went there and here and had not a problem with myself.

Stayed out enjoying myself because I thought it was the thing to do, I didn't want to miss out on anything,

Yea everything was easy and it seemed like the world was my stumping ground.

Yea...when I got upset a curse would creep out.

Was liking and loving persons that was not deserving of me but I played my part and was gullible to them and their wayward lies, and deception.

Yea...living the life without a care in the world, and looking back was out the question.

NOW...something has got a hold of me and I seem different, I still look the same but I'm not.

Now All I used to do I have NO desire to do, places I went is not even in my thoughts.

When someone doesn't like me...I pray for them!

Along this road I haven't lost anything...but I've gained something and SOMEONE so **GREAT!!**

Yea...my peculiar demeanor has directed me to seek *HIM* only and I love it! I may have strayed away from friends for a season but I'm changing for the better!

I'm trying to become ALL *He* wants of me, I'm trying to be an image of my *Father*, to ALL that may not know of *Him,* I want to witness to them,to those that knew me then(I got the last laugh),those that....

That...that judged me!

When you have elevated yourself into a new level your mind changes, your spirit changes, your desires change, and all the while you begin to change on the outside because the inside has changed.

People see you got a different walk, talk, a glow that's unexplainable, and a spirit that's **Unbreakable!**

Yep...smh the Metamorphosis is still in progress and like a butterfly I will emerge into ALL *HE* wants me to be!